Mommy AND Me

CORINNE B. TREPANIER

Order this book online at www.trafford.com
or email orders@trafford.com

Most Trafford titles are also available at major online book retailers.

Printed in the United States of America.

ISBN: 978-1-4669-8663-3 (sc)
ISBN: 978-1-4669-8665-7 (hc)
ISBN: 978-1-4669-8664-0 (e)

Library of Congress Control Number: 2013904974

Trafford rev. 03/18/2013

 www.trafford.com

North America & international
toll-free: 1 888 232 4444 (USA & Canada)
phone: 250 383 6864 ♦ fax: 812 355 4082

I wish to dedicate this book to all of my family whom I love deeply!

I wish to thank my husband for supporting me every day it took me to write this book and for being my editor. You are my blessing!

Chapter 1

It all started with one person, Otto Donau. He would shape the way his life and his family's lives would be. His life experiences compared to most others were beyond comparison. World War I is where my tale will begin . . . . Shortly after the war started my grandfather would be captured by Russian soldiers and transported to a prison camp in Siberia. He would spend 6 long years in that cold desolate place before he would escape. It changed him in ways that perhaps he wasn't even aware of. When he would return to Austria, he was extremely disciplined and had become the ultimate perfectionist. After having nothing at all, he would appreciate absolutely everything he would have. Even the smallest things he treasured and protected and that would include his children. He always dressed the best in dress pants, a dress shirt and cardigan or a suit. Otto would never leave the house if he was wrinkled. Halfway through the day he would even go home so he could iron his shirt so he was crisp and clean.

World War II was a horrible and turbulent time for so many people and their families; for those who lost loved ones and those who felt the aftermath of such an all-consuming war. There are so many directions in which someone could go with that topic and the direction I go is not the direction in which so many of you would think.

On February 22, 1943, right in the middle of this Great War, a child was born in Judenburg, Austria to Otto and Rosa Johanna Donau. She was the 8th of 10 children that were born to Otto and Johanna and she would be my mom, Ute. Sadly, one of her siblings, a little boy, would die shortly after birth. Her eldest sibling, Rosa was 22 years her senior and all of them, with the exception of three, were still living at home with their Mama and Tata. Two of those children were yet to be born and Otto Jr., as we would call him here in America, was fighting for Austria in the war. Because Austria was under the control of Adolph Hitler, Otto Jr. would be considered a Nazi, but his beliefs were far from that which the SS followed. Interesting, yes of course, how many people can say that they had an

Figure 1 Otto Jr. shortly after joining the military

Uncle who fought with the Nazis? He did what he had to do and that was it. He was a free spirit and often did what he wished.

Most of my mom's siblings who were old enough were in the Hitler Youth, a program which tried to instill anti-Semitism in the young people of Germany, Austria and the surrounding countries. As it was described to me, the Hitler Youth was a sort of boy scout/girl scout program that was a bit on the extreme side. Is that perhaps putting it a bit mildly? I've seen many documentaries on the issue of the Hitler Youth and what it meant to the 3rd Reich and what I got out of it was that it wasn't all bad. It taught children a strong work ethic and responsibility at home and in government.

The Hitler Youth organization was set up by Adolf Hitler in 1933 for educating and training male youths aged 13-18 in Nazi principles. Under the leadership of Baldur von Schirach, by 1935 it included almost 60% of all German boys, and by 1936 it became a state agency that all young "Aryan" Germans were expected to join. I believe expected is a relative term here. Was it mandatory to join or were they actually given the choice? Regardless, the youths lived a simple life with little possessions, a life of dedication, fellowship, and Nazi conformity, with very little parental guidance.

Later a parallel program would be developed for young girls. When the girls were old enough, they would be sent to live with another family to work alongside the mother to learn to cook, keep house and be a good wife and mother. I, obviously, didn't grow up in that generation. Just ask my husband and he'll tell you. Ute's mother would even have a neighbor's young girl work alongside her. Hannel, as she was called by Otto, was so happy to work with the girl. She showed her how to cook, sew and keep a good home. Where she found the time to take care of her own children, I don't know. All in all, I believe the Nazis wanted to teach these children how to be good Germans. What the definition of that would be, I do not know. I do know that Adolf Hitler wanted to teach the children about the Aryan race and what he believed was its supremacy.

At the time of my mom's birth WWII was in full swing. In early February of the year 1943, Vienna, Berlin and Munich were severely bombed. It was a war where Hitler's extreme Socialist ideals were the focus. Every legal document and political document was marked with a swastika, making sure everyone knew who and what they were bound to; the Third Reich, Hitler's cause. My mom's birth certificate even has a swastika at the bottom of it and she hates it with all her being. Of that she is definitely not proud. From fighting in Germany and Austria to fighting in France and Japan, the war was everywhere and not a single person in Europe or America could avoid its effects. Soldiers from all countries reported casualties and many of their bodies would never make it home but be buried where they fell; some in unmarked graves and others in mass graves. Like nearly every war in history there were countless men who were never found and their families would never know what happened to them. Ute unfortunately had a cousin who was dear to all of her family that was killed in action. Her older brother Heimo had in fact written a letter to the German Kaiser to congratulate him on a medal that the Kaiser had received and to ask of the service of his friend and cousin. On the following page you will see the letter he received back from the Kaiser. In English, its basic translation was to thank Heimo for the acknowledgment of the medal he received and that his cousin did not die in vain as he was a good SS soldier. For me, looking back on it, I don't know that it would have offered me any comfort at all. Yes, he was a good soldier, but he fought for a losing cause; a cause that was unjust to so many. You will notice that the letter my uncle received was dated September 5, 1943, almost 7 months after my mom was born and the clearest two words on the paper were Heil Hitler.

Ute was much too young to understand the things that were going on around her. She has told me on several occasions that she remembers the bombs going off along with air raid sirens blaring in the distance. She never said she was frightened and perhaps she was lucky that she was so young and didn't understand the dreadful events that were surrounding her. The capture of the Jews and their removal from their homes and their subsequent resettlement in concentration camps was one of the most dreadful events that were happening in the first couple years of her life. It was a blessing for her indeed not to remember, as I could never imagine having to personally witness those travesties which were committed by Hitler and the believers in his Reich. My mom did tell me that the only time she was really afraid was when her family would all sit around to listen to the radio in the evenings and she would hear the Russian language spoken. I have asked her why the Russians scared her so and she really couldn't give me an answer.

Austria was occupied by not only the French, but by the Russians and English as well. Walking down the street could be an experience all its own seeing people from several different countries occupying the place that the Donau family called their home. Food was scarce and so was money, my mom's father would make certain everyone was taken care of and had enough and her mother would make sure that everyone felt safe and loved. Every day was a struggle but one that they would come out of for the better. The year Ute was born, they moved into a building of what we would call here in America, condominiums. It was a small place with just two bedrooms but they would make it work. How they could make it work with 6 children and two adults, I will never understand. The walls were bright and light colored with stencils of tiny blue flowers everywhere. The furniture was white and the home was always kept so very clean and shiny. It was a very welcoming and happy place as my mom would describe it. They were given the apartment for free but were not permitted to sell it as dictated to them when they received it. A stipulation, I could imagine, which was made by Hitler's government.

Because there were so many of the family in just a two bedroom apartment, Ute had to share a room and bed with her sister Barbel. During the night, the living room would become another bedroom for the rest of her siblings. Otto had designed a bed that could be hidden during the day and easily brought out at night to accommodate the children. It was a tight squeeze but they were cozy together. By the time Ute was three years old, her eldest sibling Rosa would get married and move away, followed shortly thereafter by her sister Ruth and brother Heimo. There was a little more room now in their cramped little place but there were also two more siblings born into the Donau family; my mom's younger brother Edwin and the baby of the family Karin.

Otto Jr., who had been fighting in the war, disappeared for nearly a year. No one knew of his whereabouts all the time he was gone and during that time he never thought to contact his family to ease their minds as to his location. When he did finally come home, they learned that he was just wandering the country doing what he wanted, where he wanted. He was a free spirit and fortunately much later I would have the joy of meeting him.

Figure 2 Otto Jr. shown second from right with his company

Regardless of the worry that came with young Otto's disappearance, they were rich with love if nothing else. Their father, Otto, was a typesetter working for a local newspaper at the time and when he wasn't working at the paper, he would write identification cards for people out of their living room. Because of the war and Austria being occupied by three other countries, everyone had to have an identification card in all four languages. Of course, most people couldn't write in all the languages, Otto would do it for them for a small fee. He was always busy and found something to keep himself occupied all the time. Drawing and doing woodcuts were some of the things that he greatly enjoyed doing. He would go out to certain areas of Judenburg that he wished to draw and Ute would sit with him and just watch. He created masterpieces in my opinion and those masterpieces that survived were given to his children and grandchildren. As I was told, a museum in Judenburg holds several of Otto's pieces.

During the time Otto was working as a typesetter, he would develop lead poisoning and that combined with his kidney disease and asthma, he became dreadfully ill. For nearly 11 months he would suffer and Hannel would nurse him constantly while making sure her children and home were taken care of as well. Hannel was a seamstress making men's suits so she worked harder than ever to help support the family while Otto was ill. She was such a strong woman and I think my mom, perhaps, got her strength from her.

Chapter 2

U te was getting older and since the war was now over there was
more freedom for all of the family. Ute's father would become
a graphic artist so if she wasn't with him while he would draw
or just spending time with him walking in the mountains, she could be
found with her mother. One of her favorite things to do was to walk
through the woods surrounding the city making arrangements of wild
flowers and mushrooms for her mother. She took great care to braid these
flowers into beautiful little garlands that were filled with blue, purple and
white flowers as well as multi-colored mushrooms. Unfortunately by the
time she got home her beautiful little creations had nearly completely
fallen apart, but nonetheless her mother loved them. Any gift given to her,
she would treasure as if it were gold.

Ute loved to wander around the town and through the woods but she
would never go too far. There were places that she would steer clear of and
those would be the buildings and the homes that were located near the
ancient stone wall surrounding the city. They frightened her in a way that

she could not explain. She mentioned that she saw them as being so dark. I can imagine how old they must have looked as the wall that surrounded the city was centuries old; a remnant of when the city lay within the Eppenstein Castle nearly 800 years before. I think I may have been the one to go exploring that wall just to feel the "oldness" of it, to feel the history and to imagine all the stories that went with it.

They were living in a time where food wasn't plentiful and meat wasn't always on the table at mealtime. Somehow Johanna always made sure that there were small pieces of beef and potatoes with lettuce and homemade bread for each of the children. Her children's bellies would never be empty. She would make homemade horse radish sauce, not the kind found here that is creamy, but a sauce made just from the horse radish. My mom just recently told me how she loved it when her mom made it. In their household, nothing went to waste. Johanna would find a way to use whatever they had. When Ute was older she would tell me that she had to guard her plate when it was time to eat because at any time one of her brothers could rush in and steal the food right off her plate. I can imagine my mom hovering over her food protecting it from starving predator brothers.

When Ute was 3 years old, she started gymnastics and twice a week she would religiously go to practice. She worked hard at it and enjoyed it a great deal, but she never had the self-confidence to believe that she was any good. Her coaches had her always working one floor routine or another; that is where she would excel. Ute was quite disciplined, whether it was practicing her gymnastics or doing what her mother or father asked of her. It was something that her father passed down to her and possibly expected from her. She would stick with her gymnastics for many years, but other things would interest her as well. As she grew older, she would spend more and more time with her friends. She was such a social butterfly and so outgoing, the complete opposite of me. Much like her father, she said what was on her mind and did what she pleased just as long as her father approved. Well, to be honest, there were things that he didn't approve of but he didn't have to know about them.

She loved to go to school, not for the academic part of it, of course, but for the social aspect, after all she could spend time with her friends; and it gave her time to get away from her brothers and sisters. She always did well especially excelling in mathematics even though she greatly disliked her teacher. One day he made a mistake while doing figures on the blackboard. Ute, of course, noticed it right away and told him of his error. The teacher became very angry with her for pointing it out in front of the class. He yelled at her and as outspoken as she was, she called him an idiot not so quietly under her breath and of course he heard her. The next day, her principle was waiting patiently for her outside of the classroom to have a little talk. He explained to her that she could think it but not say it out loud. She told him that she was going to beat the crap out of that teacher. For the next three evenings, her math teacher would not step out of his home to water his garden as he always did, because he was afraid she would be waiting for him. She of course, had no intention of going through with it.

I remember my mom telling me on more than one occasion how she hated English and Latin and she didn't hide that fact from her teachers either. She was so strong willed that she would often get into trouble because of her hatred of the classes. In order to pass her Latin class she had to take an additional test at the end of the year or risk receiving a failing grade. Failing that class would have been horrible for her and I'm sure her father would have had something to say about it. If she could only have known that English would be the only language she would speak for most of her life.

Figure 3 Ute at a dance, fourth one in on left

Ute and her sister Barbel didn't always see eye to eye. They were the complete opposites; where Ute was always neat and tidy, Barbel was always messy and unorganized. Their personalities clashed in basically the same way. As I said, they were complete opposites. Ute's side of the room was always spotless while Barbel's side was always a mess. It drove my mom crazy as she always had to have everything in its place, but what could she do about it? She wasn't about to touch Barbel's side of the room because if she did, she'd have to deal with Barbel being irritated with her for touching her things. They were just two different people and would never get along the best. During an argument between the two, and this was by the time both Ute and Barbel were teenagers, Ute was chasing Barbel up the stairs of the building they lived in and up through the apartment yelling at one another over something that I'm sure neither remembers. Unfortunately, Barbel shut Ute's arm in a door. That was one way of ending the argument. Ute suffered a minor fracture and was put in a half cast. It was the kind of cast that was hard as a rock and went half way around her arm and was kept on by stiff gauze on the bottom. At the time of the accident she said it hurt like crazy but once she was able to move her thumb without it hurting her, she would take that cast off at every opportunity. She hated that thing. She told me of how her father yelled at her sister after the accident, "Did you see what you did? Did you see?" I think my mom might have been his favorite? I could be wrong.

Ute was getting older and spending more and more time with her friends. Boys started noticing her and she was not unaware of that fact. There was one boy who liked her whose name was Hans that just wouldn't leave her alone. He was from Yugoslavia and lived in a refugee camp at the bottom of the hill at the edge of the city. One afternoon she just had enough of him bothering her, so she just bopped him on the head with the hard part of her cast and went on her way. He didn't bother her again.

When Ute was around 14 or 15 years old, and after so many years of practicing, she participated in her city's gymnastics championship. She had become excellent in the floor routine, even though she never had the confidence to feel that way. It was her turn to do her routine and she would do it quite well. She would fly through the air doing flips and rolls on that bright blue mat always keeping her legs perfectly straight with her toes pointed just the way they were supposed to be. Everyone cheered for her when she completed her routine but honestly she didn't think she did her best. When the competition was over and all the participants had had their turn doing their routines on various apparatus, Ute was standing with the rest of her friends on the team. It was time for the judges to start giving out awards and announcing the winners. When they got to the award for first place they called Ute's name. She didn't think she had heard correctly and didn't step forward to accept. Everyone around her would say, "Ute, they're calling your name. Go. Go." She had won first place and was champion of the competition. She was given an olive wreath that she would proudly hang on the post of her bed.

Every Sunday, Ute and her father would go for a walk to take care of her aunt's grave as no one else would take the time to just stop and visit. As they would walk through the village and the woods they would stop to care for the grave, light a candle and just visit. It had become a ritual for them, something they would always share. On one instance she was caught up spending time with her friends and completely forgot about their walk. So when it finally popped into her head that it was time for their walk, she raced out of the door of her friend's home without giving them any explanation and ran up the cobblestone street to catch up with him. She couldn't miss that Sunday walk. They walked silently along that cobble stone street onto a gravel path leading to the graveyard. Once they reached the grave, both Otto and Ute would clear it of any debris and make sure the candle was lit. They wanted Ute's aunt to know that she was not forgotten and paid tribute to her in that way.

**Figure 4 Woodcut of Judenburg done by Otto Donau
in the late 1920's or early 1930's**

Chapter 3

The Donau family was rich with tradition and they treated each one as special as the next. Each person in the family participated in one way or another. There were several traditions that they held dear and all of those traditions Ute would pass on to me and my siblings. We would hold them as special as they did, I believe.

One special time of the year which was Mommy's favorite was in early December when St. Nickolas would come. She loved the celebrations that surrounded it. And then there was the Krampus who unlike St. Nickolas was a beast-like creature who would punish the children who misbehaved during the year. All the kids would put their boots outside the door with hopes of St. Nickolas coming and filling them with nuts and fruit. Each year there was a festival in the town square of Judenburg where they celebrated the event. Children would often dress up as St. Nickolas or the Krampus and go door to door looking for treats as we do here in America during Halloween. My mom would dress up and go out with her friends to celebrate in the square. There was music played and people dancing around trying to steer clear of the wicked Krampus with his willow switches and chains. They would laugh and play like children enjoying every moment of the celebration. Years later when I would visit Austria with my mom, I was able to experience the tradition first hand in her home town. To see the excitement in my mom's eyes and the smile on her face while we were at the festivities; now that was something that I will never forget. It makes me smile now just thinking about it. As I would also live in Germany, I had my own experience with St. Nickolas and the Krampus. On the evening of St. Nickolas, he and the Krampus were walking around the village that I lived in with my parents and two siblings. The second I saw the Krampus, I flew through our apartment and under my bed. There was no way I was coming out, not when he was there. After lots of coaxing from my parents, I still refused to come out because I knew I was safe under my bed.

Another yearly tradition that my mom's family had was their traditional Christmas. It started with the first day of advent which started on the first Sunday of December. On the table of their home would be an advent wreath made of local fragrant evergreen twigs with four candles equally placed apart from each other in it. The candles were usually red and in the center of the wreath would be another candle to mark Christmas Eve. On each Sunday evening of advent, they would light one of those candles and all have tea and cake while Johanna or Otto would tell stories to all of the children. It was mostly for the younger four as Barbel, Ute and her two younger siblings were called by their elder siblings. All of them would sit around the wreath listening raptly to everything their parents had to say. Advent was a treasured tradition that my mom would pass on to myself and my siblings and we loved it. We loved the smell of the evergreen twigs in the wreath my mom would make herself. The aroma filled the air and the house making us feel that Christmas was on its way. Mommy served us tea in these glass cups that sat in white and red metal frames with a handle on it. I think there were apples on those tea servers; little red apples and all those tea cups would sit on a tray that was white with those same small apples. My mom would tell us the story of the match stick girl and other stories that I unfortunately can't remember. That story was the only one I could remember as it was a bit of a sad story that stuck with my mom since childhood as it would stick with me.

On Christmas Eve, my mom's entire family would bundle up and go for a walk, usually to my mom's aunt's home and then to the cemetery to visit my mom's grandparents graves. During their walk they could see into the windows of the houses that they passed and the Christmas trees were all lit by white candles and the families that they saw were all sitting around the tree having their own celebration. At that time, real candles were lit instead of the tangled strings of lights we use today. When the family would return home, they would light their own tree and celebrate their Christmas around it. Every year Otto had to make sure that their tree was shaped absolutely perfectly and if it wasn't, he would drill holes in the trunk of the tree to insert branches so it was perfectly symmetrical. He was without a doubt a perfectionist. Their Christmases weren't about presents as they had very little. It was about tradition and the family being together; that was the most important to all of them.

The Austrian Holiday traditions from my mom's youth were so different from those that you typically hear of here in America. As the story goes, while the family was out at church on Christmas Eve, the Christkind or Christ Child would fly into the family's home on tiny little wings to light the tree and put the presents out for them to discover when they returned home. Of course this tradition can be compared to Santa Claus coming to houses in America on Christmas Eve to deliver presents. We would celebrate Christmas Eve in much the same way. All of our family, with the exception of my sister would head off to church and when we returned home, we would find that Santa had been there and placed all our presents neatly beneath the tree. On one Christmas Eve we had just returned from the candle light service at our church and when we all reached our front door, we heard sleigh bells. My brother and I got so excited and said, "Santa's here!" Much later we would discover that my sister was the one who played Santa for us during our years in Germany.

Over the New Year's celebration, the family again would all gather together to celebrate another years beginning. One of the things that the family would all do together was melt small balls of lead in a spoon over a fire. Once the lead was completely melted, they would pour that lead into a cup or bowl of water. The object of this tradition was to try to determine what the poured lead looked like after it was taken out of the water. Sometimes you would see certain shapes and if you did, that was your New Year's fortune. We still do that nearly every year and have for as long as I can remember. At the stroke of midnight, all the bells in Austria would ring to celebrate the New Year and in some areas fireworks were lit to help with the celebration. In the smaller villages, people would go outside of their homes and bang pots and pans together making all kinds of noise. When my mom, dad and we kids did that many years later in America, all we got were strange stares and shouts of "Be Quiet!" I guess all traditions aren't universal.

Another common Austrian and German tradition was Fasching. It was a weeklong celebration which began the week before Ash Wednesday. It was a time for the people to dress up and really let their hair down; to have fun. They would have a grand parade with everyone dressed up, dancing around the town and carrying lanterns. The candles in the paper lanterns would shine through the colored paper and cast different colored shapes that would dance along with the people in the streets. Music could be heard coming from restaurants and taverns and wine was drunk by most of those who participated, making the parade all the more interesting. People were laughing and singing and dancing through the streets following the parade; becoming the parade. It could be compared to a similar event held here in America called Mardi Gras. At the end of the Fasching week, the Tuesday before Ash Wednesday, a huge doll made of straw that was said to contain all the sins of the people who participated in the festivals would be burned or buried. My mom and her siblings always participated in the festival and had the greatest fun, dancing and running around through the parade. They would listen to the music and feel free spirited for one single day. My siblings and I would later get to see this festival when we lived in Germany and it was something to behold. The lanterns caught my eye and I thought them the most beautiful thing I'd ever seen.

The life that Otto and Johanna gave their family was a rich one. It was rich with tradition and love. Ute has always spoken of both her parents with such admiration and love. She shared a great affinity with her father; he adored her and she adored him. Although at times he was hard on her, she loved him dearly. All he wanted was to protect his children and give them the best lives he could.

Chapter 4

Not all the time would Otto and my mom agree. Ute loved to listen to the radio in the evening right before she went to bed but her father did not approve. He didn't like the new singers, but my mom just loved them. At night when it was time for bed, she would sneak the radio close to her bed and turn it on very quietly so she could listen to the singers she adored. One of those singers was Pat Boone. What was her favorite song? April Love! Years later, Ute would be lucky enough to attend one of his concerts. I attended that concert with her and remember how as we were ushered down that red carpet to our seats, the usher kept going and going . . . So I whispered to my mom, "Oh my goodness, I think we have front row seats!" Sure enough we were front and center and during one of his songs he came down to shake hands with some of the people. When he came to my mom . . . . The smile on her face I will never forget. She finally got to shake the hand of her teen idol. I'm so jealous, now if Josh Groban would just shake my hand. Hmmmm . . . .

At the age where she first started to adore Pat Boone was the age where all teenagers were into their music; I was no exception. They had crushes on this singer and that singer and it was no different for Ute. She wanted to put posters of her favorites in her room but that wasn't allowed. Another of her favorite singers came to Judenburg for a concert. Fortunately, after a lot of coaxing Otto would go with Ute to the concert. While she would enjoy the music, her father would quietly sleep in the seat next to her. Ute managed to find out which hotel this singer was staying at so she would sneak off and make her way there. She didn't even get close to the hotel before she was turned away. She was so close, but those who worked for the singer wouldn't let her near. Darn, how she wanted to meet this guy. She was so very disappointed but as with everything else, life would go on.

When Ute was a young teenager she got her first job in a local delicatessen. Every day, close to lunch time, she would see her mama's bun just peeking over the bottom edge of the window as she walked by to bring her daughter lunch. It became a thing that she came to expect. It was a routine that would happen every day and she would look forward to it.

Ute spent a lot of time with friends but she always had time to spend with her Mama and Tata. She greatly enjoyed just being with her mama if it was to help her cook or watch her darn socks or sew which she hated, she enjoyed that time so very much. Ute hated playing games but her mama loved it. Her favorite game was Monopoly, so on occasion Ute would play with her just so she had that time to spend just with her Mama. When she wasn't with her Mama, she could be found with her father watching him draw or sharing a walk in the mountains.

A short time later, Ute's mama would become ill. It was determined that she needed to have her gall bladder removed, so she was set to go into the hospital for the "routine" operation. I ask myself often if any operation at that time could really be called routine. Medicine was nothing like it is today. It was the 29th day of June 1958 when Johanna would pass away. She was just 56 years old and leaving her beloved husband and children behind. My mom was just 15 and devastated. She wasn't even able to attend her funeral. She has trouble talking about the loss still to this day after so many years, so I don't ask. It's something that I don't think you will or could ever get over. Her Mama was gone and she would never see her again.

Ute stayed with her father and younger siblings for another 2 years working in the same deli as she had when she was younger. When she would go out for walks in the evenings her father would often accompany her. Evenings had become their time. Otto couldn't go out during the day very often as the car and factory fumes would greatly trigger his asthma. He was aging as well and missed his Hannel terribly, so perhaps he held onto Ute just a little tighter. When she turned 17, Ute made the decision to move to Germany where her eldest sister lived. She had found a job and a place to stay with the family for whom she would work. Before she left, she and her father made a pact. When each of them would take their evening walks, they would look at the North Star and know that they were walking together.

Ute was able to go home to Austria to visit her father and two younger siblings twice over the next two years. She was doing well in Germany and had grown to really like the woman for whom she worked. But, soon, things would never be the same. In 1962, Otto would suffer what we believe was a brain aneurysm that would put him in a coma. Shortly after, he would pass away too. My mom was just 19 years old and an orphan. Both of her parents whom she so dearly loved were gone. She was at a loss as to what her life would become, so she returned to Germany to continue working for the family who had taken her in. Nothing could console her and she wasn't able to deal with her loss, so she made one of the biggest decisions in her life; one that would change her life forever.

Chapter 5

U te had a very wealthy uncle who lived in Chicago, Illinois so she decided to take the biggest leap of her life and go to America. She was running away from the sadness that overwhelmed her most of the time over the loss of her Mama and Tata. I don't think she made the decision to move to America with the thought that she was running away, it was just the only way she knew how to cope, so she would make a new life in America. With her would be her elder sister Barbel. The year was mid-1963 when they landed in Chicago. It was such a different place with different customs, a different language and different people. I can imagine the confusion and questions that must have popped into their heads as they looked around at the new world they'd found themselves in. Were they doing the right thing moving so far away from the place they grew up in and was so familiar to them? They made their way to their Uncle's house to start their new life.

Their uncle wasn't the nicest person in the world, so nothing would be given to them. My mom never expected a free ride and would have gladly repaid anything she was given. All they were given was a place to stay and in most cases they weren't even allowed to shower inside the house, but had to shower outside. They were in a big city with houses so close together; I can't even imagine how uncomfortable that must have been. Ute found a job in a German Delicatessen and later a German Bakery and would start a class to better her English so that she could become a citizen as soon as she could. She was busy in a new world, working, learning English and making a new life for herself. She tucked away the pain of the loss of her parents as best she could, and forged ahead.

Figure 5 Ute shortly after she moved to America

Not long after Ute had established her life in America and found her own apartment with her cousin from Austria, she would meet a young man who would sweep her off her feet. She was smitten by him and him by her. He was from India and was very charming and handsome. In mid-1964 they would marry and it seemed they were very happy. He treated her so well, as my mom would tell me. Occasionally he would ask if she could go shopping for him as he needed clothes for a cousin of his who was still living in India. She happily did so, brought the items home, packaged them up neatly and shipped them off. She often did this for her husband and was happy to do it as he explained to her that his cousin didn't have much in India. During that time, she would become pregnant with her first child. She was overjoyed at the coming of her child, but something had changed in her husband. Ute couldn't quite figure it out and tried to put it out of her mind until he decided that she should go back to Germany until she gave birth.

Figure 6 Ute in a Temple Garden in Chicago 1964

Ute did as he directed her to do and went back to Germany to live with the same family she had worked for a few years earlier. One great thing she was happy about was she was back at home where her family was close. It made her happy to be with her family but there was something in the back of her mind that just wouldn't let her be. In all that time, she hadn't heard a word from her husband.

In June of 1965 she would give birth to her first child. She was on her own in the hospital with no one there to give her support; until she saw her little girl. She was so beautiful and had the darkest hair. That little girl would become Ute's entire life and all she would live for. When her daughter was about three months old Ute would make her way back to America; back to the apartment she had before she left. For over two years she wouldn't see her husband nor would she hear a word from him. Finally, not being able to understand what had happened, she wrote a letter to India where she believed he was. What she would find out would rock her to her very foundation. She would find out that the October before they had married; he had gone home to India and married another woman. He was already married when he married Ute! What shock and devastation she must have felt. The clothes that he had her buying were not for his cousin but for his wife. She was buying clothes for her husband's wife!!! How could things possibly go from bad to worse; the death of her parents to the betrayal of her husband?

This was something all new that she had to get over and with time she would, for the most part. Working hard to move on she would later find a good job at a large television ratings firm that would just pay enough so she could support herself and her precious little girl. The apartment she lived in was small but just big enough for herself and her little girl. She worked hard to make it as comfortable as possible for them both. My mom told me a story about her trying to refinish the floors in the apartment. She had rented one of those large sanding machines and didn't quite realize what power it had, she would end up sending it right through her wall. Her landlord was very understanding and helped her to fix the wall.

During the day, her daughter would go to stay with her sister Barbel and her husband so that she could work. Her little girl was very happy spending the days with her aunt and uncle and their dog Rex. It was like a second family for her and since Barbel didn't have any children of her own, my sister would get spoiled. She would make many memories with them. Although Ute made barely enough money to pay the bills she would always find a way to make things work.

On Sundays, to make a special day for her daughter she would take her to the free zoo in Chicago, or for a walk through one of the large department stores downtown and out for a hotdog. It was such a simple treat for them both but they treasured those outings. Ute had made a life for herself and her daughter and they were happy. She wouldn't hear from her husband until a couple of years later.

When Ute's daughter was just a couple of years old, she received a call from her attorney letting her know that they had received word from her husband and needed her to come to their office. She had no idea why he would be in contact with her attorney so she went ahead to his office. What she would hear when she was called in would push her beyond anger; beyond disgust; beyond belief. Her husband and his wife were unable to have children, or so they believed and wanted to purchase Ute's daughter for $10,000. Ute shouted out a few expletives, which she never did, and said, "Never in a million years." Furiously she stormed out of that office. Her mind was racing, her heart was beating nearly out of her chest; she was beyond angry. She was insulted! How could he possibly wish to buy her daughter and take her away? Never! And so, she would never hear from him again. Never would she receive support in the form of money of any kind or even a letter asking how their little girl was.

Chapter 6

Life would go on for Ute and her little girl. Ute had made several great friends at her job and she would often bring her little girl into her office. The girls would all ooh and ah over her and spoil her as everyone else did. How could they not? My sister was the cutest little girl I've ever seen. One of the friends she made at her job was named Marianne. They became close friends and would go out for dinner now and again with the other girls they worked with and they had even planned a trip to Glidden, Wisconsin to visit Marianne's parents. They had a good time getting away and it would seem that Ute was accepted and liked by all of Marianne's family.

When they returned to Chicago, life would return to normal. Ute would go to work and pick up her little girl from her sister and go home. It had become their routine and Ute remained focused on her little girl. She was all she had and lived her life around her. Her friend Marianne had planned a dinner to try to set her brother up with my mom's niece who was very close to her in age. Ute was also invited to the dinner but didn't expect what would happen. At the dinner she met Marianne's brother Johnny. Ute liked him right away but didn't make a move to let that fact be known. After all, she was still married and unknown to her so was he. Although she liked him she let things go and after the dinner just went home. After all, she had her little girl to think about.

Sometime later, Ute would receive a phone call from Marianne and Johnny's mother. In that conversation Johnny's mother said that she was afraid he was going to get away and that Ute should talk to him. My mom was unsure how she felt about getting involved with someone but she would contact him. They went out here and there; going to farmers markets or just out for a simple meal. Johnny, having returned from two tours in Vietnam had found a job at Midway Airport which was quite a distance from where Ute lived. So, they spent a lot of time speaking over the phone. Ute was falling in love.

Not soon after Ute and Johnny started dating, he would re-enlist in the U.S. Air Force. To her utter dismay Johnny received word that he was going to Vietnam for his third tour of duty. The previous two tours he had volunteered for, and this tour he would do the same. He felt it was something he had to do. Ute was devastated and terrified that Johnny would be in the midst of a war where he could easily be killed or captured. Every day, all kinds of thoughts would go through her head but she would try to be as strong as possible. She had to be for herself and her little girl. During the year that he was in Vietnam, Ute and Johnny would write to each other every day and send audio tapes back and forth. She would even wear a pair of his old fatigues so she could feel closer to him. They kept in constant contact the best they could. For nearly the entire time that Johnny was away, Ute was a basket case. She would hear on the radio or TV of casualties in the village my dad was stationed in and she would become hysterical. Her co-workers would try to reassure her that it wasn't him and if it had been she would already have been informed. She wasn't so sure. Her nerves were as frayed as a worn rope. It was during that horrible time that both Ute and Johnny would get their divorces and Ute would become a US Citizen. As soon as Johnny would return from Vietnam, they planned to be married. Thankfully Johnny would return home safely.

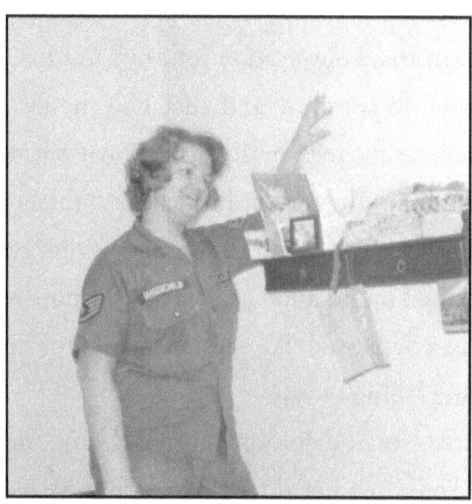

Figure 7 Ute in what she would call her favorite spot while Johnny was in Vietnam

Around March 1, 1971, Johnny made it home to Chicago and a week later on March 7, they were married in a small ceremony. Johnny would wear his dress blues and my mom would wear a pink Asian style dress. It was simple but beautiful and exactly what they wanted. Johnny's brother Bill and his wife Jackie would stand up with them. The entire wedding would be planned by Ute's sister Barbel and after the wedding they would spend their honeymoon in Glidden, Wisconsin, where Johnny's parents lived.

Since Johnny was still in the Air Force, he knew that he would soon receive orders as to where he would be stationed next and sure enough; within a month he received those orders. They were to be sent to MacDill

Air Force Base in Tampa, Florida and happy was not the feeling that my mom felt. She hated the thought of Florida with its palm trees, the heat and the bugs. It was someplace that she would never have wished to go. Before they received their orders to go to Florida, they had actually put in for North Dakota and at the last moment those orders were changed to Florida. So, Ute, Johnny and Ute's little girl would pack their things up and move down to Tampa. Johnny had come to adore Ute's little girl and she would adore him as well; they had become a real family.

Shortly after moving they were finally getting things settled when Ute would discover that she was pregnant with her first child with Johnny. They were both extremely happy to be having a child, but my poor mom had morning sickness from the moment she discovered her pregnancy to the moment she delivered. Ute's little girl, my sister, was excited that she was to become a big sister. On January 29, 1972, nearly a year after they married, my mom gave birth to my brother John Jr. or Hansi as we all would call him. He was a healthy little boy and my sister loved to care for him. Since my sister was an only child for so long, my mom made sure to include her in everything with her little brother; from feeding him to bathing him or just putting him to bed.

As Hansi grew, he and my sister would play in the front yard of the building where they lived. Their home which was on the second floor of a building on base faced Tampa Bay. In the small yards surrounding the building they would see jack rabbits running around constantly and they would both go chasing after them. My mom once said that she was afraid of those rabbits because they were so big. My sister didn't care; she was fearless. So while chasing those rabbits my brother would be close behind joining in on the fun. When Johnny's schedule would permit, the family would pack things up for a picnic and go to the beach so my sister and brother could play in the sand and enjoy the bay. Mommy was a stay at home mom most of the time so she was always doing something with her kids. The only drawback . . . . She couldn't drive.

Very soon after Ute gave birth to Hansi, she became pregnant again. When she was about four months pregnant she suffered appendicitis. From the surgery, she would develop a staph infection and would spend at least a week in the hospital. A very long week as she would describe it. Shortly after she returned home, Ute went back to the hospital telling them that she was in labor. It was way too early and Ute knew that but she was sure she was in labor. Unfortunately, the nurses didn't believe it was labor she was experiencing. She had already had two children so I think that she would have known whether she was in labor or not. Shortly thereafter, as my mom lay alone in her hospital bed she gave birth to a little boy. He was very tiny, but my mom would tell me he looked just like Hansi. Sadly, he lived for just a few moments and died in Ute's arms. She had his first breath and would have his last breath as well and I would hope that would give her a little solace. That moment, among the so many other devastating moments she experienced in her life would stay with her forever. They would name that little boy Micah Reinhold and he would never be forgotten by his siblings or his parents. Does a parent ever get over the loss of a child? I think it's something that stays with them the rest of their lives. Every August 25th, which was Micah's birthday, I try to spend at least a little time with Mommy to maybe distract her from her hurt. Ute never knew what happened to her little boy, as they took him away soon after his birth and unbelievably never let her know what they did with him! So several years later I contacted the base where the family was stationed to obtain her military medical records. I waited and waited for that manila envelope to show up in my mail box so I could maybe give my mom some answers. Unfortunately, it didn't give us definitive answers as to what happened but we did later find that he was buried. He was put to rest and that gave my mom a small bit of solace.

In January of 1973, Ute would become pregnant with me. She had told me at one point that had Micah lived, she and my dad, Johnny, wouldn't have had another child. So, sometimes I wonder, do I have a little bit of Micah's soul in me? I do believe that he is in Heaven with my mom's Mama and Tata and is loved and taken care of by them. But soon, my life would begin. On September 24 of that same year I was born. My mom said that I looked just like a peach and when people would stop to look at me they would say the same; until I opened my eyes . . . . Well, there's a whole other story there. I was born legally blind. I don't think that Mommy was too worried as she loved me no matter what. As I grew just a little older and was learning to eat, I ate by texture. My mom would have to put everything in the blender with sugar and into a bottle with a larger hole in the nipple so I would eat. She would also leave Cheerios around here and there so that I would pick them up when I would get hungry. Mm I loved Cheerios!!

Chapter 7

About a year after my birth, Mommy and Daddy took me to the hospital near their house so I could have an operation to correct my eyes. I was so little that I don't remember a thing, which honestly was the best thing they could have done. I wouldn't remember the trauma of a surgery. She would tell me that from our house on base, she could see my room and in the middle of the night she would see the light go on. Of course she was worried to no end so when she came the next morning to see me she would ask why my light would go on in the middle of the night. The nurses told her that I couldn't sleep and that one of the orderlies adored me, so he would pick me up and walk me around the hospital with him. Apparently I adored him too because I was perfectly happy with him. He was a 6 and ½ foot tall black man that was as sweet as any man could be. So many days I wish I could meet him and thank him for his kindness to me. Needless to say, when I came home from the hospital, my mom had one heck of a time getting me to sleep because all I wanted was to be carried around.

After my surgery, I do remember seeing double figures here and there. I was so little; I'm surprised that I remember anything at all. But my mom was always there comforting me and taking care of my brother and sister as well. She had a way of making me feel well when I was sick just by being near me and I still feel that. After having to wear a patch on one eye for some time, I was able to see fairly normally but would have to wear glasses. You'll hear all about how I felt about glasses later.

Mommy was always near doing something or another with us and where you would find her, I was there with her. If she wasn't cooking and baking, then she would be playing with us and telling us of her life before we came along. She would tell us of her mother and father and how she adored them. Throughout our lives she would tell us all about her parents and we would treasure those stories. Although they had long since passed away, she helped us to feel like we knew them. With my father working so often, she was alone with us most of the time. My father was quiet and not super involved; but he adored all three of us to be certain, but he wasn't the typical dad to take my brother out to throw ball or teach us how to ride a bike. But he was always there to provide for us and make sure we had enough. He always showed he loved us in one way or another. One of the memories I have of my dad when I was very small was sitting in our old vinyl recliner together eating carrots and watching TV.

By the time I turned two, my brother was 3 ½ and my sister was 10 and my father would get new orders. My mom and dad put in for three places and received word that they would be stationed at Plattsburgh Air Force Base in Plattsburgh, New York. So the family was on the move again. We were perhaps lucky in the fact that the military packed us up and moved all our things for us so all we had to do was board the plane and go. Yay, my mom was away from Florida and the yucky bugs and palm trees. We were going to a place where we would have a real winter, something that my mom always loved.

My mom got us settled in a house that my parents had purchased off of the Air Force Base. She was always the anchor for our household, putting everything in its place and making sure we had a happy home. I don't remember a whole lot about New York but a few things here and there. I remember that we had yellowish carpet that was shag. It was the typical carpet of that time. You just have to love the 70's. I also remember sitting on our cement carport in the summer time with my sister and watching her painting my toenails red. I remember how it made me feel. I was so little but felt so glamorous with red toenails. What a thing to remember?

During one of our first winters in New York, my mom decided she wanted an ice skating rink in the back yard so she did it. Of all the things that she could want, she wanted an ice skating rink. So she flooded our back yard and turned it into her own personal ice skating rink. She loved to skate and now she had it right in her back yard. I have a few memories of that too and believe me they aren't good ones by any means. I remember that the rink and the back door to our house were connected; if you will. There was a slight hill and I do mean slight, which went up to the back door. I couldn't skate at all and hated the cold and I remember trying so hard to get inside the house but I just couldn't get up that stupid tiny incline to the door. I would try and just slide right back down again and again. I cried and cried waiting for someone to come get me. Thankfully, Mommy came and got me before tiny little me froze.

I do believe my mom was happy in New York. I think she felt comfortable there and that it was slightly comparable to her home in Austria. My mom and dad would pack up us kids once and a while and take us to Vermont or to Canada on a mini-vacation. It was a time for my dad to get out of uniform and my mom to get away from everyday life. Mommy described Canada to me as being so beautiful and later would describe the architecture of Quebec to me. In my imagination I created a place of splendor with tall buildings with magnificent steeples. To me it was a kind of fairytale land. These were just some of the images that popped into my mind. Whether Canada was how I imagined it or not, I have no idea as I have no memories of being there and I haven't been back there since.

Every year my mom would make that ice rink in our back yard and would skate quite often. I, as I said, hated the cold so I stayed inside. I was so unlike my brother and sister who were always outside playing in the snow and creating a sledding run at the side of our house. They would get so mad at me because when I was outside; I just stood there and didn't move. I wanted no part of sledding and even less with the snow. One other memory that comes to my mind was a day that my mom came in from skating still wearing her skates. I was standing behind her but she didn't realize it as I was still so small. Well, she took a step back and stepped on my big toe with her skates. It was a great tragedy to me. I thought my toe was going to have to come off! I remember riding to the hospital in our white station wagon with blue vinyl seats just staring down at my toe and crying like any 3 or 4 year old would do. Of course, it wasn't as bad as I made it; just a really good gash that required butterfly bandages. I still have a small scar that will always remind me. How horrible Mommy felt that she stepped on my toe. I still tell her that it wasn't her fault and it was just an accident after all.

Four years after we were moved to New York, my dad received new orders. These orders, my mom was more than thrilled about. We were moving to Bitburg Air Force Base in Bitburg, Germany. Mommy was going home and would be able to see her family again after so many years.

Our first year in Germany, we lived in a little apartment in the Village of Koosbuesch which was just a short drive from the base. As I said, the apartment was quite small with slanted walls to accommodate the roof line, but we had a balcony, which I thought was so cool. My mom made good friends with our neighbors and of course with the people they rented from. We called him Opa and his wife Oma and they were forever giving us kids little gifts. The gifts were either cherries from their tree or simple candy treats made at the store up the road.

My memories grow sharper now as I've gotten just a little bit older. We also lived next to a pig farmer who we all had great fun hanging around. My brother, who was about 8 years old by this time, seemed to have a real connection with that farmer, Heir Heinen. He would ride on the wheel well of his tractor and they would talk back and forth. So what was the trouble with this? Heir Heinen didn't speak a word of English and Hansi didn't speak a word of German but a jolly time they had. My mom would often go with me to visit the farmer because I was still quite little. It was all so interesting to me and I had to go see the animals. We would crouch down on the ground, take a spade and dig up the dandelions in the yard so that we could feed them to the pigs. We just loved feeding the pigs it was so much fun for Mommy and me.

We had another neighbor whose name I only remember as Renate. I would often go with Mommy to visit her. We would sit at her table with a tiny cutting board in front of us and eat open faced sausage sandwiches with a knife and fork. I thought that was the coolest thing ever, just as long as there was no mustard or mayonnaise. During one of my mom's many visits with Renate, Hansi and I would hide behind their raspberry bushes and eat to our hearts content. My mom never knew until many years later that we did that. She was so shocked when she found out, I never knew why she felt that why. Maybe it was because we were for the most part really good kids.

I started at a German Kindergarten in the village of Koosbuesch when I was just 4 and I hated it from the moment I walked in to the moment I walked out. I wanted to be with my Mommy and she wasn't there. Not to mention, they all spoke German and I didn't understand a word they said. I felt as though I was in a bubble with everyone talking around me and their words were just bouncing off of the bubble I was in. I felt so disconnected from everyone around me and the discomfort that I felt was something I can't really describe. One day, my mom thought I was ready to go to school on the village bus on my own. I was still really scared, which was a normal state of being for me, but she reassured me and told me everything would be okay. That didn't matter; I was still scared out of my mind. I was afraid of everything. I remember sitting across from another little girl who was blonde and looked so nice. She tried talking to me and I felt so uncomfortable because I couldn't understand anything she was saying. Once she realized that I couldn't understand her, we rode along quietly for what I thought was a long time when the bus broke down. There we sat and waited and waited until another bus could come and get us. I never told my mom about that until years later. I knew that she would feel horrible for sending me on the bus to school that day.

We had so many good times in Koosbuesch. To this day, certain smells remind me of the walks we used to take in the village. The smell of a new rain, earth worms and diesel engines from the local tractors, they all bring me back to the days that we would walk through the village. I know that those things are strange things to trigger memories but I remember those smells so clearly from Koosbuesch.

After our first year in Germany, we moved onto the Air Force Base into base housing. I remember it at first as being a very sterile environment with cement stairs leading up to our fourth floor apartment and white walls everywhere. The building we would live in would directly abut a soccer field and I remember on occasion watching the kids all playing soccer. I also remember that my brother and I had to share a room and that the room was huge. We were both young but my mom came up with the greatest idea to give us both our own space. She would put up a curtain dissecting the room with rollers on it so that we could separate my side from Hansi's side. There was a playground very near our building and most important of all, there were American Schools on base. I would be able to understand the other kids and my teachers. But overall, school terrified me.

The summer before school started, my brother and I noticed that there was a circus putting up their tents directly across the road from the building in which we lived. Hansi had to go check it out and of course I had to follow him. The circus was just on the edge of the base but not on base, so we weren't supposed to go over there; not to mention that we weren't supposed to cross the busy street to get there. I remember all the colors of the tents and of course all the nasty smells of the animals. Yuck! Well, my brother got a job cleaning up after the animals and I, well I got a job too. The nice men would sit me atop a big log and I would supervise. I was really good at it! Mommy was so upset when she found out that we went over there.

When it came to being away from my mom, I would have such an overwhelming fear of being abandoned, of being left behind or lost. I don't know where that fear came from and honestly it doesn't make any sense. All I wanted was to be with my mommy and forget the rest of it. On my first day of American Kindergarten on base, I was terrified. I was crying like I never remember crying and I just didn't want to go into the building. Just thinking about it now makes my stomach do flips. My mom of course walked me and my brother to school with our great big book bags, but I didn't want to let her go. At one point, I made her promise that she would stay with me and she did, but she had to stay outside of the classroom. I remember looking up at the door of the room and seeing her through the small glass window and feeling like just taking off and going to her. Looking back now, I wonder, maybe I was afraid of losing her like she had lost her parents when she was so young. Was that why I was so afraid of everything?

Mommy gave me everything I needed. She comforted me and made me feel safe. Going to school the first few days was horrible and I can still remember it like it was yesterday. I even remember the smells of the school room. It was the smell of crayons and chalk and to this day, those smells trigger memories of how terrified I was my first few days of Kindergarten. Things didn't get any easier for me, so the Principal of our school called my mom in to talk with her and try to figure out a way to help me acclimate to the change. His suggestion was that I stay home for a couple of weeks and try it again. Great suggestion, but it didn't work. The bottom line was that I had to go to school without my mom, so one day she dropped me off at my class room and stood outside the door for a while. Once she saw that I was being kept busy with something, she slipped away and went home. At first when I saw she was no longer there, I panicked a little but I knew I had to stay, so I just did what I had to.

It was at this time that I got my first pair of glasses and of course there was only one choice of frames to pick from. The ones that made you look like a witch. I hated them, pure and simple. Once I started walking to school on my own, I would find the nearest garbage can and throw those glasses away. My parents always went to retrieve them so I got smarter about the situation. I would show them! What I would do was wait until right before the garbage man would come and throw them away then. Ha! That was the end of those darn glasses! Not really, but eventually I would learn to deal with them and yes, the frames would get better.

Other than going to school, yuck, yuck and double yuck, our family would travel often. Mommy and Daddy would pack all of us up into our tiny brown Volkswagen Rabbit. We would go to my Aunt Rosa's in Zweibrucken and stay with her on occasion. Her husband, my Uncle Hugo who spoke no English, would always talk to me as if I understood. He would just talk and talk and I would just smile, having no clue what he was saying to me. He was so kind to me and so was my Aunt Rosa I loved them dearly. Often when we visited them, their two children who were a bit older than my brother and I would play with us, little goofy games, but we took an instant liking to them.

We traveled around Germany quite often and although I was so small at the time I remember so very much. I remember the incredible architecture of the ancient cathedrals and I remember being able to feel the age of the ancient structures. Even then the great big churches impressed me. During our car rides, of course my brother and I either fought or played, either way, we got on my sisters last nerve. That I do know for sure.

On one of our trips, we traveled into Belgium to see where the Battle of the Bulge took place. My dad was such a fan of General Patton that we had to go see where this great battle had taken place. I remember a lot of stone but other than that . . . . Not much else . . . Kind of sad to think about really, I saw the place where the Battle of the Bulge took place and I can hardly remember anything about it. Luckily we have pictures that can infuse my memory with information.

Figure 8 my brother Hansi and me during one of our trips.

Most of our more interesting travels we made while we were living in Germany. How could we not? There were so many things to see and so many places to go that were within driving distance. We had to see them and we had to visit my mom's family. That was the best part of all. We traveled often into Austria to visit Mommy's other siblings. One of our more memorable trips was to visit my Uncle Otto. He was such a character and although I didn't understand most of what he said, we laughed so much. Every time he would greet or say good-bye to my mom he would salute and say, "Heil Hitler!" He only did it because he knew how angry my mom would get at him. Those times for him were long passed and all of his family knew that he was never a true blooded Nazi. Uncle Otto loved to tease my sister as well. We would all be sitting at dinner at a nice restaurant and you know those glasses of water they always give you? Well, he would take out his teeth and plop them into his glass of water. I can still see the scrunched up look on my sister's face every time he did it.

Figure 9 an ancient Cathedral in Vienna

We traveled to see my aunts Ruth and Karin in Graz and of course went to see my mom's hometown of Judenburg. On some of our outings my aunt Karin would come along, especially when we visited Judenburg. She grew up there too and although there were some bad memories attached to the place, there were good ones as well. We were able to see my grandparent's grave and the graves of our other relatives; those my brother, sister and I never met. I adored my Aunt Karin, although we couldn't have a conversation because of the language barrier, I just loved her. She would call me her little hex and that I will remember forever.

During our stay in Germany, my father received a message from his family in Wisconsin; his sister was marrying and he was going to go and I was going with him. I remember being excited about the trip and looking forward to seeing my grandparents again whom I barely knew. The first plane we boarded was the biggest cargo carrier made by the U.S. Air Force. This was by no means a passenger plane and wasn't meant to be comfortable. The plane was that typical military green and my dad and I sat in small metal seats that faced each other. Because the plane was so extremely loud, we had to stuff some pink goo that had a similar consistency of silly puddy into our ears to dull the incredible roar of the engines.

There is very little that I remember from that trip so it can be summed up in two words. It sucked! I missed my mom so badly for one and when my dad went to the reception I cried the whole time. There was nothing that could comfort me, although my grandma did try her best. I guess I was afraid that my dad wasn't going to come back for me. It's a crazy thought that I had because there was no reason for it because my parents were ALWAYS there for me and my brother and sister. We never went to a babysitter or daycare so whenever we weren't in school we had my mom and dad always.

I am unsure as to whether it happened on this trip or an earlier trip to my grandparents, but there is a memory that I have that I cannot forget. I must have been naughty or something because I got in trouble. I had these small leather sandals that I loved and wore all the time, well my grandmother picked me up and took me over to their black wood burning stove and opened the burner lid. First of all, I was scared stiff of that stove to begin with. I remember seeing the flames dancing around in the stove and felt the heat on my face as I looked down. As I watched, she dropped those shoes into the fire and I had to watch them burn slowly until there was just a glimmer of what they used to be left. I was traumatized at the burning of my shoes and never understood why she did that. This story I hadn't told my parents until very recently. I am sure my grandparents loved me in their own way but I never felt it and I really wanted to as they were the only grandparents I had.

When we returned from Wisconsin, I remember riding in the cab to the building we lived in. There I saw my mom pacing the sidewalk and as soon as I saw her I swear I almost jumped out of the car before it even stopped. I was beyond excited to see her and she me. I swore, even though I was so little, that I would never go away from her for that long again. And believe it or not I didn't; not until my honeymoon with my husband 20 plus years later.

Chapter 8

O ur family had spent four years living in Germany and unfortunately, it was time for us to move again. Although my memories are a little sketchy of our time in Germany, I remember it fondly and the memories I do hold, I hold dearly. My father received orders that he was to be stationed at Columbus Air Force Base in Columbus, Mississippi. We knew the orders were coming so we weren't surprised that we would move again. So off we were. The move didn't really faze my brother and me too much. It was just a new adventure. The Air Force packed up our things and shipped them along with my parents brown VW Rabbit to the United States. It was cold when we left Germany so we were all dressed accordingly, boy were we surprised when we landed in Charleston, South Carolina. Holy moly it was hot!!!

We were able to pick up our tiny brown car and start our drive over to Columbus, Mississippi. Since my Mom didn't drive, my dad had to do all the driving. We three kids were oblivious to all that went on in the front seat because we were busy playing or fighting as we always did on trips. We made one stop in Georgia to spend the night at a hotel before we continued on our trip. We all were so excited because there was a pool and we got to go swimming. Yay!

The three of us kids got all suited up and went to the pool. I loved the water but there was one big problem, I couldn't swim. I got on the ladder and slowly climbed down and before I knew it there wasn't another step and I was under the water. I remember seeing the ladder clearly and trying to get back on it but I couldn't. Lucky for me, my brother saved the day. He reached in, grabbed me by my pony tail and pulled me by the hair out of the pool. Thank you Hansi but ouch!!!

The next day, we started the final leg of our trip to our new home or so we thought. When we arrived on base in Columbus, my father was told that our home on base was not ready for us yet. Well, oh good. So we got back into the car with all our baggage and went to a hotel. We weren't sure what to do from then but we were assured by base housing that they would find us a place to stay until our home was ready. And they did, boy they did. We pulled up to this trailer park that was in one of the scariest neighborhoods of Columbus and we got out in front of this mobile home like house that was up on cinder blocks. My mom was so disgusted she didn't know what to do with herself, clean it or demolish it. We had no choice so we unpacked our things and tried to settle in as best we could. That was until the night came.

That was when the creatures came out. The biggest, leggiest, grossest cockroaches I have ever seen in my life and will ever see I can guarantee! During the night, as we slept we could hear them climbing the walls and scurrying from here to there. I don't even want to know how many of them climbed all over us as we slept. What I don't know won't kill me right? Yuck! That's all I can say about that place, no good memories there. Then during the day, the sound of the cicadas was deafening.

My brother and I started school at a place called Franklin Academy. I would start the third grade and my brother would start fourth. When we walked in the first day, I felt dwarfed by the place, it was palatial and everything was marble. The sounds of the voices echoed throughout the building giving it an eerie feel and unwelcome feel. Every morning Mommy would walk us to school and pick us up afterward. My sister would start her junior year of high school at Leigh High and would ride the bus to get there. It was so very hot, that on our walk home, mommy would take us to this small store for a small treat, an ice cold Coca-Cola slush. They were the best thing I remember of those walks home from school. We have yet to find Coca-Cola slushes that tasted as good as those.

Soon, before we were dragged away by the cock roaches, our house on base was ready and we moved in. My brother and I stayed in the same school as did my sister. The difference was we were in a little community; a military community that we loved. During the summer, which was actually most of the year, we would go swimming at the base pool. That's where I finally learned to swim. My brother and I were always together going to that pool and having the greatest fun.

It was our second year in Mississippi when my mom finally learned to drive and once she got her license, there was no stopping her. She took us everywhere. We would go for rides just to go. At about the same time, my sister was learning to drive as well. My dad had gotten a black VW bug and was teaching my sister to drive it. I was standing in the driveway of our home when my sister started to pull in the driveway. All of a sudden, all I could see was the bottom of the car. No, I didn't get run over, but my sister did one heck of a wheelie with that VW Bug. Needless to say, I will never forget what the bottom of a car looks like. It was also the time that my parents bought a house outside a small village named Caledonia which was not far from the base. It was an old plantation house called the

Dale Mansion. Don't let that name fool you, it was not a mansion by any means. It was a two bedroom home with two living rooms. One of those living rooms my brother and I would share. We would have such fun in and around that house. Hansi and I would wander through the woods and ride our bikes to the local river to go swimming. There wasn't a place near our house that we didn't go to investigate. We would run into the remnants of slave huts as we were later told and a tiny little house that sat directly next to our house passed a great big fence. The tiny house had long since been abandoned and was falling down. The wood was weathered and splintered and foliage was growing through the roof. The curiosity of course got the better of us and we went in to check it out. Spooky is the only word I can use to describe it. It was as if the people who had lived there just walked out and left everything behind. It gave me the creeps.

The bad part of moving to Caledonia was that we would have to start another school and we all know how much I loved school. Luckily, I had my brother to rely on a bit. Whenever we moved, I knew I had at least one friend in Hansi.

During our first year in the school at Caledonia, the middle school caught on fire. It was the biggest blaze I had ever seen in my life and honestly, it scared the wits out of me. All the kids were running away from the building and the fire and I felt confused and lost until I heard my brother screaming for me. We were loaded onto a bus along with tons of other kids and taken safely to our homes. I remember the melted windows of the buildings that stood next to the burned structure and the trailers that were moved in to school the middle school kids. There was nothing left of that part of the school.

After we moved into the house outside the village of Caledonia, my mom started a job on the Air Force base. When we were in school, it wasn't so bad, but when the summer would come, I hated that my mom had to work and we were home alone. Hansi and I always found something to do whether it was inside or in the upper level of the shed that stood next to our house. Hansi had decided to make a fort out of the second floor of that shed and we would spend a lot of time up there.

My sister was mostly out on her own doing her own thing. She was finishing her last year of high school and was always busy with this or that activity. We didn't have much of a relationship with her at the time because we were just too young and she couldn't relate to us. Soon, after we moved to Caledonia, our big sister would go off to college. It was a little strange for me seeing her room empty and not seeing her come and go. I used to go into her room and sit and look around just trying to get to know her a little. She gave me her robe before she left and I treasured that tattered old thing like it was made of gold. Sounds stupid, I know, but it was a little bit of my sister that I could connect to. I wanted so much to be just like her. She was outgoing and popular and knew exactly what she wanted out of life. I envied that greatly!

My brother and I were always so close and were finishing our 6th grade year when my dad made the decision that he was going to retire from the Air Force. He spent 27 years serving our country and thought it was time for him to become a civilian. I think Mommy was worried a little bit as we had all gotten so used to the military community and the perks that it had brought us but she would get used to the idea as we all did. After all what choice did we have?

Chapter 9

After getting used to the idea of becoming a non-military family my mom and dad made the decision to move back to the place that my dad had grown up. Mommy had such a hard time with this move as we were going to be leaving my sister behind. She had to let go of her little girl and get used to the idea of living so very far away from her. Mommy never showed much emotion or worry to us but I knew that she had to hurt leaving her first born on her own.

After packing things up and saying good-bye to the great friends we had made over the years in Mississippi, we set off on the long trek to Wisconsin. I was more excited about leaving than I was sad about leaving friends behind. It was a new place for us and a new start. Plus, we would be near my dad's family and get a chance to really get to know them. Before the decision was made to move to Wisconsin, my dad was told that there would be plenty of jobs for the taking once we got there. Unfortunately, for a man newly retired from the Air Force who worked in civil engineering for years, no one would hire him. Although he was a plumber for years, the Air Force didn't require him to be licensed and not being licensed pretty much doomed him for finding a job.

I remember how my mom worried and how my dad went everyplace he could applying for jobs. Sometimes, we would go with him and sit outside in the lobby while he would go in to fill out the applications. For weeks, nothing came his way so he would eventually settle on a job working for a place specializing in the care of mentally challenged children and adults. He would refinish furniture there and get paid barely enough to support four people. Although my dad did receive his military pension as well, we had very little and some of the nice people we met knew that and helped out with gifts of meat or vegetables here and there. My mom was so very grateful to them but it was hard on her worrying where the money would come from to pay the bills as they came in.

Mommy loved the area in which we lived. It was a tiny town in the North Woods of Wisconsin surrounded by miles and miles of woods. She loved to walk in those woods and cut evergreen boughs to make her own wreaths. She hated our circumstance but loved the area. She and I would go for rides through the back roads and fire lanes that surrounded Glidden and just enjoy the sights and smells of the evergreens that surrounded us. Glidden was known as the black bear capital and on one of our rides we would see a black bear and its cub crossing the road. We were both in shock and just sat there in the car and watched as they crossed in front of us. We were scared and in awe at the same time. Why we were scared, I don't know as those bears were more scared of us than we were of them.

Soon both my mom and dad would get night jobs working at the local wreath factory. I remember I could see the old factory from the window in our living room and I just watched, waiting for my mom to come home. I missed her. That was the time that we got cable and I was glued to MTV taping videos and watching constantly. It was a bit of company for my brother and I having cable.

Again, though, we had to start a new school. I was extremely shy to the point of being painfully so. Having Hansi with me to start our new school was again a comfort. Like several schools before, I always knew I had one friend when we started. Once I got used to going to school, things got better but the financial situation wasn't changing.

During our first year in school in Glidden, the high school started on fire. It was an extremely old building and burned like nothing I've seen before. The flames and smoke could be seen for miles. Everyone watched the fire from a small diner that was a block away. The flames took up the whole skyline and everyone was in awe. The first question we had to ask? Were we cursed? Just a couple of years earlier our school had burned in Mississippi. Spooky and scary were the feelings that we had and our friends shared those feelings with us as well.

Although I hated school, I made some great friends that I will never forget. I would spend most weekends with one of my best friends who lived on the lake. We would go swimming and watch scary movies. We had so much fun. On one day as we were walking down the road near her house I saw a strange looking stick, so I picked it up. I never threw anything as fast as I threw that thing. The darn thing wasn't a stick, it was a snake. It scared the living crap out of me but we laughed for hours over it. She and I had so many great memories and I treasure all of them.

I also met a boy there whom I liked so much but the shyness in me also made me scared of him. Crazy, I know but I was in crazy like with him but couldn't do anything about it. We "went out" for a short time but because of my fear it didn't work. That didn't mean that I still didn't like him, I was just too afraid. I was so young at the time. I was in the 8th grade and soon would be moving again.

Chapter 10

We would spend two years in Glidden before moving away. My dad was in a dead end job and had to do something to support his family. He would apply and be accepted to test to work for the Department of Corrections. At 45 years old, my dad was embarking on a new career. He worked so very hard to get this job. There was a requirement in order to get into the academy and that was to run two miles in a certain amount of time. My dad ran and worked out so he could make that run. I remember he wore a light grey sweat suit as he ran and would come home all sweaty and worn out. He did it for us and moved to Oshkosh, Wisconsin to start the academy. We were so proud of him. It would be a good job for him and change things greatly for us. After he graduated from the academy, he came back to Glidden for a short time before he moved ahead of us to Waupun, Wisconsin so he could find us a house and get things a bit settled before the rest of us moved.

It was 1987 when we all moved to Waupun. My mom seemed happy in our new home and would also find a job at the local florist and wreath making factory. Hansi and I would be starting High School and I was terrified. It was school and my history of hating school continued. I was painfully shy and didn't quite know how to act around these new people I would meet. I was so afraid that I would never fit in. Since I was so shy, I was never the one to approach someone to introduce myself to them and that made me feel so socially inept. If they didn't come up to me, I kept to myself and did what I needed to do. Just four years. It was like torture for me. I did make some great friends but I also developed a lot of resentment for those who never gave me a chance. It's a stupid feeling to resent someone for not getting to know me. How were they to know that I was so very shy and scared to death of my own shadow most of the time?

The one and only time I approached someone was our freshman year. I was sitting with my brother and the guys he was getting to know when they started talking about something gross. I had noticed a girl who was sitting on the opposite side of the room and decided, okay, I'm going to do it. So I went up to her and asked her if I could sit next to her. She looked at me a little funny but said sure. Marsha and I would become best friends and that friendship still continues after nearly 26 years.

High School, for the most part was a horrible experience for me. Walking down the halls between classes, I felt so uncomfortable. I went through the odd stages like everyone does and dressed pretty much the way I was feeling. Dark clothes and strange hair with the Cure T-shirts and Chuck Taylor's, that's how I looked for the first couple of years. The last couple of years, I had lost a bunch of weight and dressed more "normal." I had a few boyfriends here and there, even the boy from Glidden that I liked so much, but none of them would last. I suffered heartbreak like every teenage girl does. It's a fact of life and something that I would get used to.

By the end of high school, I was so ready to be away from all the people and uncomfortable shyness I felt that most people didn't know about. Graduation couldn't come soon enough for me, but graduate I did. Yay, high school was over.

In the fall I would start my first year of college. Honestly, I spent more time partying than going to classes. I pretty much failed the first semester and decided to start working. I knew I had to go back to school, but I was just having so much fun. During the time just before High School graduation I started dating a guy named David. I really like him and he really liked me, but I was at a stage in my life where I just wasn't ready for him. My mom adored him for the most part but I just couldn't stay with him. I had things I wanted to do and experience and I just couldn't do those things with him. He and I would remain friends, thankfully and he was always there for me when I needed a shoulder to cry on. After an ex-boyfriend beat me pretty badly, David was the first one I called. There was something in him that I was drawn to but there was also something that scared me a bit from the start. He had a little girl.

A year after I failed terribly out of the first college I went to, I went back to school to become a legal secretary. It was school and of course I hated it like every other school I attended. The thought of having to be with new people and try to become comfortable around them was the hardest part. Although I was so shy and uncomfortable around new people, I always managed to make friends and they were good friends to me. I went the full two years but quit 4 credits shy of my associate's degree. That would be something that I would regret many years later.

After twelve years of partying and cramming so much life into a short period of time, I would marry David. He was the one for me all that time and I just didn't know it. One of the best things I've ever done was marry him. Things aren't always easy, but I know that I have him to come home to everyday and that makes me happy. And the little girl he had, I grew to love her like my own. My brother would also get married in 1998 and his wife would give birth to two beautiful children. My mom and dad's only grandchildren and they were adored the moment they entered the world.

In March of 2011, my mom and dad celebrated their 40th wedding anniversary at a small restaurant in Illinois. The whole family was there to help celebrate. Jackie, who had stood up in the wedding was there as well. My dad's brother Bill had died many years earlier. My parents had made it through all the good and bad times and good and bad places and were still together. At my wedding I was so proud when the DJ asked who out of the crowd was married the longest and the answer was my mommy and daddy. I hope to be able to celebrate my 40th anniversary with my David.

So, after all the hardships and devastation that my mom went through, she managed to raise a family who adores her like no one else in the world. We respect her and admire her for all the things that she endured in life and are all so very blessed to be able to call her our Mommy! The life and stories she gave us made us who we are today and shaped the way we would live our lives; just as our grandfather Otto's experiences would shape the way mommy would live her life. I try to think of the things that I would change in my life if I could and there are so many. I am still as shy as I was when I was a little girl but have more strength to get past that shyness and put myself out there.

Life continues and all the memories I have of my life, my mom's life and the lives of her parents I hold very close to my heart. And now, I have shared some of them with you.

Figure 10 Picture of Statues taken in Vienna, Austria